Michael Harkavy is a global media consultant advising on film, TV, book publishing, music, and interactive entertainment. His career spans 40 years in book publishing as an editor, author, publisher, and consultant. He was a senior executive at Warner Bros Entertainment where he held the position of Vice President of WB Worldwide Publishing, Kids! WB Music and WB Interactive Entertainment. He later held the position of Senior VP of International Content and Creative Affairs responsible for strategic planning of international children's television.

He is the author of *101 Careers: A Guide to the Fastest Growing Opportunities, The 100 Best Companies to Sell For, The Brooklyn Adventures of Tommy and Mikey (a novel), The Looney Tunes: Two Nights Before Christmas,* and editor-in-chief of the *Webster's International Encyclopaedia*. His collected poems, *I Create As I Speak,* will be published in 2024 by Austin Macauley.

He is the father of Juliana and August Harkavy.

Rabindranath Tagore

Juliana & August Harkavy

Fiona Godwin

Paula Allen

Michael David Harkavy

I CREATE AS I SPEAK

AUSTIN MACAULEY PUBLISHERS™

LONDON • CAMBRIDGE • NEW YORK • SHARJAH

Cover image from the Webb telescope courtesy of NASA.

Ordering Information
Quantity sales: Special discounts are available on quantity purchases by corporations, associations, and others. For details, contact the publisher at the address below.

Publisher's Cataloging-in-Publication data
Harkavy, Michael David
I Create As I Speak

ISBN 9798889106661 (Paperback)
ISBN 9798889106678 (ePub e-book)

Library of Congress Control Number: 2023922390

www.austinmacauley.com/us

First Published 2024
Austin Macauley Publishers LLC
40 Wall Street, 33rd Floor, Suite 3302
New York, NY 10005
USA

mail-usa@austinmacauley.com
+1 (646) 5125767

The author would like to acknowledge *The Book of Songs (The Shijing)* and the poets Enheduanna, Sappho, Rumi, Dante Alighieri, Charles Baudelaire, Arthur Rimbaud, Walt Whitman, T.S. Eliot, Joy Harjo, Natasha Trethewey and David Whyte.

Author's Preface

There are many important perspectives on the origins of poetry. There seems to be a general consensus that the origins are pre-historic and relate to the sounds emanating from the planet, surrounding atmosphere and those created by various human cultures in the form of music, songs and storytelling.

What I find most fascinating about some of these opinions is the compelling thought that humans have an inner poetic voice. I believe that there are a variety of inner voices that are activated and accessed through the events of human existence.

It is my deeper belief, however, that the inner poetic voice is the secret garden of every individual's spirit and soul. It is a source of wonder, revelations and self-awareness only achievable by the sounds and meaning of poetry. It is a transformative gateway to unknown paths that reside within us all.

I Create As I Speak is the product of my inner poetic voice and my desire to share this path with others.

"Stray birds of summer come to my window to sing and fly away.
And yellow leaves of autumn, which have no songs, flutter and fall there with a sigh."

Rabindranath Tagore
Stray Birds

"…all poems are an emblem of courage and the attempt to say the unsayable…"

David Whyte

"Daylight is good at arriving at the right time…"

George Harrison
"All Things Must Pass"

I
In the Beginning

CHILDREN ARE ANSWERED PRAYERS
IN A TEMPLE YET TO BE CONSTRUCTED

THE CHILD IN YOUR ARMS
IS THE UNIVERSE WITHOUT VASTNESS

15

PUT A CHILD'S HAND ON YOUR HEART
INHALE DEEPLY
EXHALE
SAY THANK YOU

KNEEL AND STARE INTO THE EYES
OF A CHILD
PROMISE TO TELL THE TRUTH

II
Love and Other Mysteries

The Patriarch

My presence, a state of grace
Divine gravity illuminated by diminishing time
Chosen seer of faith bestowed
The invisible fragrance of flower inhaled
Becomes eternal memory
Patriarch embraced the inseparable mystery
The universe expands your being
Sing magical songs of the rebirth of ritual
Picasso hallucinating in a cave painting
What is the meaning of a petal?
Patriarchal wisdom is a vision of love and prayers
You create as you speak

God
Here are the answers for the flowers you send
Sunlight does not choose one petal
Or a stray bird
It illuminates without hesitation or preference
Dawn is the morning prayer of nature

God captures the laughter of small children
Sprinkles them in rain clouds
As we pray skyward

Memories are not yesterday
Reborn every day as a babe in swaddling
Fragile with the future in every moment

Praying voice of a woman
Absorbed by darkness in a medieval cathedral
Her faith in the cold stonewall echoing her words

Wildflower Seeds

A whispered prayer answered
Wildflower seeds tossed into the infinite heavens
Awaken to a new day
A second sun on the horizon
Around which nothing orbits but your soul
A light that creates no shadow
Newton's gravity redefined
The universe a Shakespearian stage
A newborn bard
The future cradled in your arms
Many questions with one answer
Useless metaphors evaporate
Ineffable thoughts
God has touched you
Your life in the hands of a child
Who knows not your name.

25

To all women
I kneel in the cathedral of time
Speaking prayers of gratitude
For all the tomorrows that you create

I see
Snow on the mountain
Reflecting the diminishing light of my soul
Dim silence hears the song of stray birds
I rejoice

Confident snowfall
Smiles coldly at the spring
Seeks life as water

Wind Elegy

We are fallen leaves
Earthly hieroglyphs
Secret roots of eternity
Each breathe a prayer
Every child a cathedral
I walk alone unknown
A sentient path
Destination in absentia
Meaning an unopened gift
Darkness illuminates the soul
Horizon upon horizon
Walk with me
Hold my aging hand
Silence stares
Memories breaking waves
Embrace my airborne words
I will return

29

The beauty of fragility
Is brevity

Leap eyes closed
Through the waterfall in your heart
Sightless courage of the soul

Passion
Is the gravity of love
The heart measures the distance between lovers
Time the illusion of the imagination

Invitation to an Unknown Woman

Through a small window pane
Of an insane asylum in France
Van Gogh saw a star-filled night
Cork-lined walls
The solitude of darkness in a Parisian bedroom
In pursuit of lost time
Sleepless Proust wrote
"Imagination is responsible for love"
Minds dwell in one world
Hearts in another
Entrenched in habits
Other worlds need other eyes
We will never meet in this world
Ignite your imagination
My poem is an invitation

The night is a stage
Upon which stars and planets
Perform Twelfth Night
Insouciant comets in astral aloofness
"Journeys end in lovers meeting."

Beijing winter night
Emperor's lover in jeans
Hard Rock in the snow

What we see in each other
Is the shadow of love
If you could see yourself inside of me
Shadows yield

Timid Fingertips

Beijing Saturday night
Hard Rock Café through pale taxi glass
Dreams of a Forbidden City lover
Ancient paths of a Ming god
Shards of irregular divine ice
Reflect timid fingertips touching
Pungent incense atop Imperial Courtyards
Meaning disintegrates like Lotus petals
My soul is a starless mariner
With maps of other heavens
Futility of questions
I embrace the secret meaning of things

Beaver pelts on breasts
Embraces in dim night fire
Iroquois lover

How Close

Outside the star-lit walls of Babylonia staring at the roof of
creation
Shepherds could not feel the weightlessness of your breath
on my neck
Nor the gravity in your eyes as I embrace your face
A universe of eternal distances brings you close
Orbiting eclipses
Unpredictable wonders
Ancient towers built toward heaven
Circular stones of time
Mayan astronomers measure dawn in your smile

Ancient Chinese lovers
Stand on opposite sides of a river
Reciting love poems

The Mail Arrives in Tenochtitlan

Morning sunbeams piercing fading night
Lazy darkness embraces the empty house
Your letter rests on aged Pennsylvania pine
With a 29-cent stamp bearing the word "love"
I stand atop an Aztec pyramid
Holding the envelope aloft with both hands
My feathers and jewels gleamed in the dawn light
The blue-eyed jaguar stretched across the altar
The letter now offered to my *nagual*
These are not mere words
The jaguar now has black eyes
I look at the sun
I kneel before the truth
I leap from the summit
Soar above the morning
Ximochia (wait)
Campa in timohuica? (Where are you going?)
Tlein motech monequi? (What do you need?)
Macamo xiquiza (don't leave)

Wedding Poem

Chart your journey
Fling old maps and rusty sextant to the wind
Night stars cannot guide your vessel
Fear not shadows made by the sun
Relentless waves break toward the shore
Sightless Heart the true navigator
The rising sun outlines a new horizon
Steer straight with hands locked together

The Death of a Woman
I Almost Married

Mystic voice of memory whispers
In my restless, timeless sleep
She appears
Smiling, staring, leaning toward me
I ask if she remembers
She smiles again
An awakening within
Torrents of melting spring snow
She comes closer
Out of darkness
Illuminating my room
I ask her to stay
She smiles again and touches me
Like a prayer, she says
I will always be here
I will always be here

III
Bridges and Birds

The expansion of the universe
Is in every breath I take
The destination remains unknown

The path
I travel is not a barrier
It is the entrance to my universal self

We are all stray birds
Seeking meaning as we wander
The truth is in the journey

Wild Dreams of a
New Beginning

After centuries beneath the sands of Persian minarets
And the apostolic footprints
Suburban Transit snakes along the Jersey oilfields
Past submerged telephone poles in murky, black water
In the spectacular blink of an atomic eye
Token booths liquefy and drain into the soil
Where George Washington marched to Trenton
The horizon ripples like a fast-forwarding film
Of a blooming petal on a frozen night
All is gone

The Great Kiva
Now stands above the tomb of the Bagel Express
The braids of the medicine man's son reflect in the
moonlit purple night
War canoes in the Hudson River
The carapace of a pre-historic turtle emerges in the deserts
of New Mexico
Painted warriors spears in hand dance around giant flames

Ancient volcanoes of Valle Caldera spewing
In the dim light of my seat
I struggle to find my place on a page

49

The music of dawn
Circumnavigates the spinning planet
Beethoven's dream has come true

Music is a sound god
Our ears, hearts, and minds
Are cathedrals

Music is the religion of history
Century upon century
Our faith, hope, dreams, prayers, and tears
In a cathedral made of sound
We also pray with our ears

Every Step A Bridge

Bridges with Cyclopean Stones are spirit bridges
Emerging from unknown past and present shadows
Map-less destinations
Every breath an awareness
Every step a bridge
The Universe, bridge of the unknown
Memory, bridge of time
Time, bridge of eternity
Every step a bridge
Womb, bridge of creation
Love, bridge of caring
Pontiff, bridge of divinity
Every step a bridge
The future, bridge of imagination
Your footprints are in your soul

Words
Are wounded warriors
In a timeless battle within ourselves
The timidity of expression in retreat
Make your thoughts flowers

Speech is a windblown rope bridge
Rattling in the night
Truth is still the final word

Stray Birds Still Sing

If I should die
Say no parting prayers
Stray birds still sing
Death hath no seasons
No flight path in eternity
Speed of sound unhinged from math
Sunrise Sunset
Heavenly theatre of the stray bird
Heed the call of silent wings
God hath no answers
In the flight of whispering birds
Listen Rise Descend
Stray birds still sing

Falling autumn leaves
Windswept into oblivion
Nature's Proof of the future

Ancient Siege Engines

The hero does not fall asleep waiting for immortality
Launch the ancient siege engines of your soul
Storm the redoubt of fear
Stride through the rubble
Bond to the earth with fierce talons
Humanity takes root in your vision
There is no atlas of fear
No GPS of courage
Depart in the moonless dark of memory
Universe filled with eternal light
Is awash in darkness
Separation is not a wound
Create your path and destination to the unknown

The sunrise of other worlds
Sings to stray birds
Beckoning to fly through a new dawn
As they pursue the *hejira* of flight

IV
Sadness & Shadows

How far is far away?

Solitude
Is an empty cathedral
Where your prayers echo into the universe

Moonlit winter glass
Sad soundless antiquity
Ancient Druids read

Things As They Are

Emotional atolls in a sea of regret
No sextant
No atlas of the soul
No spiritual GPS
Your North Star is not a direction
Karma, a memory navigating time
Apologies, misgivings Karmic ornaments
Repair, a journey
Not a fix
The infinite in a time capsule
No darkness, no light
Awareness is a form of generosity
Kindness an opportunity
Things as they are

Unanswered prayers collect quietly in the heart
Like old toys in a forgotten trunk

Sorrow sleeps hidden in trees
Stray birds fly from branch to branch

The sadness of all things
An eternal poem of tears
Suffering the fury of the infinite
Quiet prayers in a small church
Lord protect the whispering voices of children

In the Shadow of Shalako

Down the road from the Avon lady's trailer
The medicine man's son carves alabaster gods
I heard the tale of the giant spider
Now all roads lead to Zuni
Snaking west through pinon-swept hills
Past soaring evergreens
30 miles from the center of the world
I have come in my Toyota
To see the dance of the giant Shalako
Mesas rise like reluctant Leviathans
The blazing purple haze of sunset a solar shawl
Ankle bells of an ancient god jangle in the night frost
Chanting gods in October
Zunis pray for the Corn God's cooperation
While the Dude in the L.L. Bean shirt
Loads his camcorder
In the shadow of the Shalako

Sadness
Is a flower
That seeks the sunlight of hope

Spring snow
Melts in the soil of my soul
What you see in my eyes
Is the first flower of love

The Tenth Muse

Infinity no longer resides in the palm of our hands
Sacred rivers and mountains
Mere streams and hills
Kyrie Eleison
Prayers evaporate for the return of a muse
In an ancient mountain desert
The forearm of the last muse
Inscribed with Blake's "Jerusalem"
Gleaming eyes in a pet food store
A modern Sappho
Kind and unaware of eternal forces
Inhabiting her soul

Wisdom is a rejected gift
Listen to your children
They are the gift-givers

The man cleaning car windows
At a red light in Brooklyn
Took no money
He gave me his blessings

On the map of tragedy
Beyond sadness
Is a lake of frozen tears
Rivers of memory
Valleys and mountains of sorrow
Yet we are not lost
Faith is the Sherpa of our souls

Death in January

William Blake's tomb in Westminster Abbey
A handful of centuries from Edward the Black Prince
Perhaps it is the gilded, vaulted ceiling and stained glass
That gives death such majesty to kings and poets
The gravedigger's shovel mocks Twelfth Night
Crystal flakes of sadness celebrate Candlemas
Blanketing eternal rest
I'm tired of death in January
And the fragility of old friends
There is no glory or grace in the frozen winter earth of
January

Death is a door with no key
Gateless gate

The Ocean of life
Surrounded by the shores of death
Why do waves break toward the beach?

Grenade

Pvt. Reddick would be a grandfather today
Fort Polk hand grenade range
An adventure story for two little boys
Eyes popped when Grandpa made the booming sound
Every swinging Richard was tight
Drill Sargent brief
Pull the fucking pin
Fling it over the fucking wall
Hit the ground face first
Or go home in a body bag
You motherfuckers got that
Deathly silence
Reddick pulled the pin and pressed the safety lever
But dropped the grenade
Bugler played taps
M-16 fixed bayonet stabbed into Louisiana soil
Helmet atop stock shined combat boots at attention
Private Wilson escorted his body home to Chicago
Motherfucking grenades

V
Dreams and Moon dance

83

If you tell a child
Your mom is a gorilla
You make a new friend

A child in the darkness of night
Lost in reverie
Strokes a mother's face
Surrenders to the sanctuary of sleep

Sweet Evidence

The immortality of birthday cakes
Immune to the ravages of time
Time a tasteless ingredient
Divided into equal shares
I count the candles slowly
Eyes of the child are wide open bulging
Eyes of the elderly closed in prayer
Sweet evidence of the one true miracle
Awaits a candle in a cake

Winter shutters flap
Ladybug on toothpaste tube hears
The sun goddess laughs

If trees are prayers
The fiber of their beings
Should not become Bibles

Christmas Tree

Christmas tree roots silent memories
The first Christmas Remembered
When the last Christmas appears on the fading horizon
A crescent sliver of retreating sunlight
Warm memory ignited
Green and red bulbs illuminate the interior treescape
Crooked pine branches mesmerize a child's wonder
Gathering of the faithful
Small candles in small hands
Sing at midnight outside the doors of an 18th-century
Dutch church
The First Coming is a memory
The Second Coming a Prayer

89

Melting snow in the rain
Haruki Murakami
Poet eats steaming udon

Miles Davis "So What"
Lazy Manhattan darkness
"Kind of Blue" Broadway

One More Moon Dance

Moon torch lit
Shrouded in wispy, veiled black clouds
A widower of the universe
Remembers the forgotten
Moonbeams push passionate waves
An earthbound goddess in a dune castle
Awaits the embrace of lunar light
Leaping on the crest of waves
Rivulets of salted tears
Breach the castle wall

Abracadabra
"I create as I speak"

Dreaming With Voltaire

Leave your words at the garden gate
Sound like a relic with no flower nor fragrance
Ancestors of Persian algorithms
Cruising Lago Como in Lambos
Trespass not, silence herein
Trails unmarked
Pray to get lost
No way out but in
Do you sense your creator?
Rest in the shadow of your dreams
Awaken to new colors
Cultivate your garden

I Am Not Done Yet

I raise not the banner of solitude
Nor worship at the altar of loneliness
Even the uninvited and forgotten belong
Embrace mystery
The first step of reality
My solitude a sacrament
Like the universe
I am not done yet
Discovery is the DNA of the universe
Every life is a pilgrimage
Determination unnecessary
Your soul contains the conclusion
So
I will love when I love
I am not done yet

Cage of Time

I want to marry
An ancient Chinese princess
Who resides in a three-thousand-year-old poem
Gathering asters on the shores of little islands
Cicadas chirping into the wind
She awaits a prince on horseback
With a saber on his waist
Blessings of a good harvest
In the eternal cycles of the flowering planet
I want a pardon from the cage of time
Return to the shores of a hidden river
Where she plays a red flute
Shoeless in a brocaded robe
Forbidden to stare at rainbows
I am breathless when she bows her head and smiles

Aftermath

What is the aftermath of a dream?
I sheath its' beauty in my soul
Waves of memory retreat like an ebb tide
In a pavilion
a harnessed goddess
Eyes piercing
Through mythic dreams
I seek a lost path
Where I once held her hand
In a dream long ago